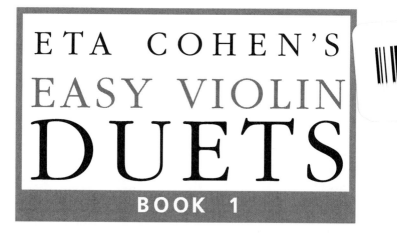

ETA COHEN'S
EASY VIOLIN
DUETS
BOOK 1

Written and arranged by Christine Brown
Edited by Eta Cohen

Novello Publishing Limited

Exclusive distributors:

Hal Leonard
7777 West Bluemound Road, Milwaukee, WI 53213
Email: info@halleonard.com

Hal Leonard Europe Limited
42 Wigmore Street Maryleborne, London, WIU 2 RY
Email: info@halleonardeurope.com

Hal Leonard Australia Pty. Ltd.
4 Lentara Court Cheltenham, Victoria, 9132 Australia
Email: info@halleonard.com.au

Order No. NOV916184
ISBN 0-85360-761-3
© Copyright 1997 Novello & Company Limited.

Music set by Stave Origination.
Cover design by xheight design Limited.

Music set by Stave Origination
Cover design by xheight design Limited.
Caligraving Limited, Theford, Norfolk

CONTENTS

FOREWORD

These very easy violin duets will fill a gap in the repertoire of beginner violinists. As soon as pupils can play very simple tunes they will find great joy in playing with others of the same standard.

Playing these duets will encourage pupils to listen to the playing of their partner as well as themselves. The score format helps awareness of the two parts, and as they are of equal difficulty it makes the interchange of parts easy. The dynamics give a clue as to which part should be prominent.

The simplicity of the duets will also allow pupils to concentrate on posture and intonation – so important at the beginning – and if the pupils are encouraged to use whole bows and play with strong firm tone, these pieces will prove a good foundation for further development.

These duets have proved very popular with our own young pupils. They can also be played by groups of violinists and would make attractive concert items.

Eta Cohen & Christine Brown

1 PIZZICATO PRELUDE

Playing pizzicato enables you to concentrate on your left hand.
Always listen to both parts and see how they fit together.

2 WOODLAND WALTZ

Play this gracefully, imagining the dancers.

Christine Brown

3 NORWEGIAN SPINNING SONG

Think of a spinning wheel and keep the music moving.
Use half bows for crotchets and whole bows for minims.
Notice that only the second violin is playing pizzicato.

Traditional
Arr. Christine Brown

4 ALLELUJAH

Play majestically, keeping the bow near the bridge to produce a good strong sound.

Use whole bows for minims and half bows for crotchets.

Traditional
Arr. Christine Brown

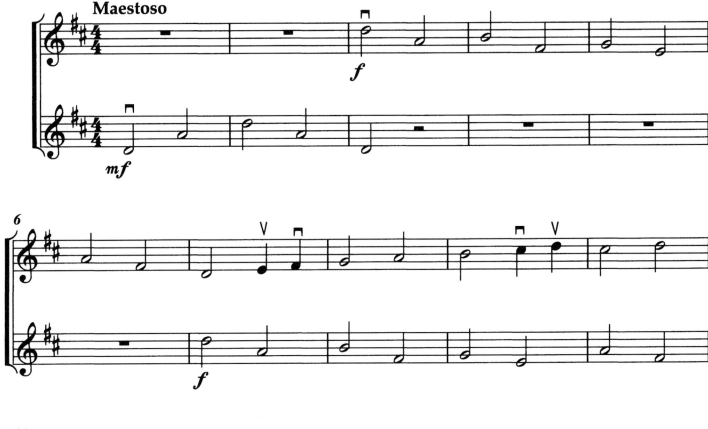

5 CHINA ROSE

This is a gentle piece. When you play ♩. ♩ make sure that your up bow is swift and light.

Christine Brown

6 SLEEP, MY BABY

Play as though you are rocking a baby to sleep.
Use whole bows in every bar.

Christine Brown

7 GRASS SO GREEN

This is a cheerful piece. Play vigorously, using plenty of bow.

Czech Folk Song
Arr. Christine Brown

8 EVENING BELLS

Use half bows for crotchets and whole bows for minims and dotted minims.

Traditional
Arr. Christine Brown

9 FRENCH CAROL

Play smoothly and make this lovely melody sing.

Traditional
Arr. Christine Brown

10 SOURWOOD MOUNTAIN

Play with energy and firm rhythm. Use short bows
for crotchets and quavers and whole bows for minims and semibreves.

American Folk Song
Arr. Christine Brown

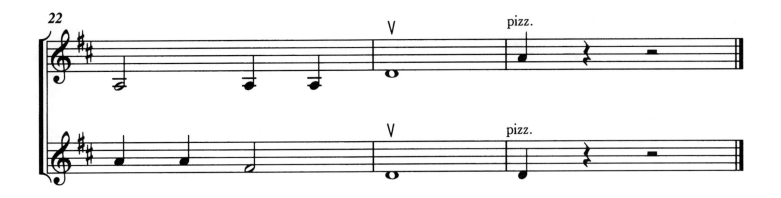

11 GAELIC MELODY

Play this piece calmly and expressively.

Traditional
Arr. Christine Brown

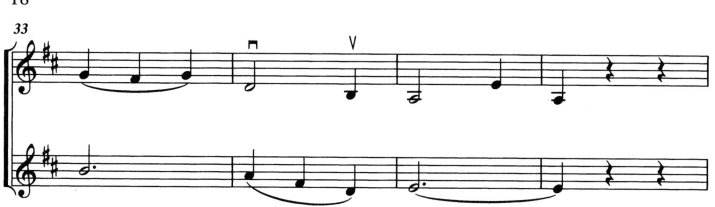

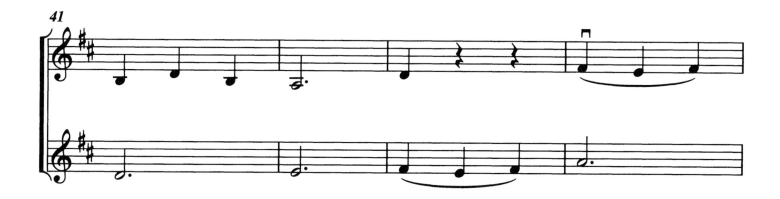

12 THE DRUNKEN SAILOR

Play with great spirit, using short bows for both crotchets and quavers.

Traditional
Arr. Christine Brown

ETA COHEN'S
VIOLIN METHOD

This highly respected violin course is the first choice for teachers in the UK and abroad. It includes the following material:

STARTING RIGHT

Covers the vital preliminaries to playing for the young beginner violinist, enlivened with colour illustrations. Includes accompaniment parts for violin duet and piano. (NOV916176)

BOOK 1

Student's Book (NOV916136) Violin part with teacher's notes. Divided into 30 Steps, each introducing a new technical point.
Accompaniment Book (NOV916137) Contains the piano accompaniments.
Teacher's Book (NOV916175) Violin duet parts and notes.
Learning to Play the Violin Three cassettes (NOV916167-01/02/03) and an instruction book (NOV916167) designed to accompany Book 1. The recordings provide the piano accompaniments and second violin parts.

BOOK 2

Student's Book (NOV916170) Every exercise and piece in this book is designed to improve and introduce new aspects of technique.
Accompaniment Book (NOV916171) Violin duet part and piano accompaniment.

BOOK 3

Student's Book (NOV916172) 30 graded lessons introducing technical points gradually, supported by numerous pieces.
Accompaniment Book (NOV916173) Contains the piano accompaniments.
Teacher's Book (NOV916174) Violin duet part.

BOOK 4

Complete Book (NOV916177) A wealth of valuable repertoire and studies which develop vital new areas of study. Includes violin part and piano accompaniments.

YOUNG RECITAL PIECES

Supplementary material for the Method books 1-4: three books of enjoyable pieces for young violinists, including many well-known works in easy arrangements. Each book contains the violin part and piano accompaniment.

Book 1 (NOV916180)
Book 2 (NOV916181)
Book 3 (NOV916182)

EASY VIOLIN DUETS

Ideal for group teaching, introducing ensemble playing and making the early stages of learning more fun. These duets are carefully graded to be used alongside Starting Right and the Method books.

Book 1 (NOV916184)
Book 2 (NOV916185)
Book 3 (NOV916186)

Novello Publishing Limited